CONTEMPORARY
CRAFTS

CONTEMPORARY
CRAFTS

KATHERINE SORRELL

This is a Parragon Publishing Book

First published in 2006

Parragon Publishing
Queen Street House
4 Queen Street
Bath BA1 1HE, UK

Copyright © Parragon Books Limited 2006

Created, designed, produced, and packaged by Stonecastle Graphics Ltd

Text by Katherine Sorrell
Photography by Jackie Skelton
Designed by Sue Pressley and Paul Turner
Edited by Gillian Haslam
Diagrams by Malcolm Porter

ISBN 1-40546-722-3

Printed in China

contents

Introduction

Forget misshapen ceramic pots, hairy macramé and lumpy sweaters in outrageous colors—modern craft is sleek, sophisticated, and highly desirable, whether in the form of jewelry, personal accessories, or items for the home. This book aims to offer something for everyone who is interested in craft, whether a complete beginner or a more experienced maker. These designs have been devised by experts in their field—makers whose experience has allowed them to modify traditional, sometimes complicated, professional processes, into easy-to-follow projects that are satisfying to produce, easy to live with, and beautiful to look at. Though some may require a small investment in equipment and materials, they are all essentially very affordable, allowing you to make gorgeous things without breaking the bank. What's more, no special work studio is required, as each project can be carried out on a kitchen table, in a spare room or, in some cases, while sitting on the couch. No particular skill is required to tackle any of the projects, just an open mind, enthusiasm and a little dexterity. So why wait? It's time to stop reading, and get making. Enjoy.

floor pillow

YOU WILL NEED

*To make a pillow measuring
   30 x 30in*

Pair size 19 (15mm) knitting needles

21oz extra-chunky yarn

Scissors

Large-eyed, blunt-ended sewing needle

Pins

Tapestry yarn to match the knitting
   yarn

Backing fabric in suedette or other
   sturdy fabric, measuring at least
   40in square

Sewing machine

Sewing thread to match your yarn

Four large snap fasteners

Sharp sewing needle and thread to
   match your yarn/backing fabric

30 x 30in pillow form

Floor pillows are both stylish and practical, useful for extra guests and ideal as a comfortable support for a quiet afternoon's lounging around. This version is quick and easy to make, with a backing made from suedette or any other sturdy fabric that won't mind being scuffed around on the floor and can be washed easily (snap fasteners are used so the cover can be easily removed). The top is knitted up as four squares, using the two basic stitches, knit and purl, so it is very straightforward. The large stitches, made by using chunky yarn and over-sized needles, are in proportion to the size of the pillow, and there's a nice decorative feature in the form of the raised, visible seams. A neutral gray has been used here, but choose any color of yarn that suits your room, remembering that paler colors are likely to get dirty more quickly; if you like, you could mix two or four complementary colors to create a fashionable patchwork effect.

floor pillow

1 Cast on 25 stitches. Knit one row and purl the next. Repeat, until you have made a square. Bind off, leaving a 6in end. Repeat three times to make four squares each measuring roughly 15 x 15in. Sew the ends of the yarn in.

2 Lay the squares out flat, with the knitting rows running in opposite directions. Take two of the squares and pin them wrong sides together. Using the tapestry yarn, backstitch along one seam, about 3/8in from the edge, making a visible seam. Sew the other two squares together in the same way, then sew the two rectangles together to make one large square.

3 Cut the backing fabric to the same dimensions as the knitted square, but allowing 3/8in on one side for turning in. Pin the knitting and the backing right sides together. Machine stitch around three sides, leaving a seam allowance of around 5/8in.

4 Turn in the fourth edge of the suedette 3/8in and hem. Sew on four snap fasteners at even intervals, and stuff with the pillow form.

BLOCKING YOUR KNITTING
A technique called blocking is an excellent way to smooth the final appearance of your knitting. Simply dampen the fabric, pin around the edges onto an ironing board (or a padded flat surface), and gently steam iron before leaving to dry.

gossamer scarf

YOU WILL NEED

To make a scarf measuring
62 x 5in

Pair size 19 (15mm) knitting needles

3½oz eyelash yarn – in a
variegated color

Scissors

Large-eyed, blunt-ended sewing needle

Ultra-fashionable once again, knitting has undergone a renaissance in recent years, becoming the favored pastime of Hollywood A-listers such as Gwyneth Paltrow and Julia Roberts, and appearing on the catwalks in various modern guises. No longer lumpy, frumpy and out of proportion, knitting is now fresh, exciting and highly desirable.

Not only is this delicate scarf absolutely gorgeous, but it's also ridiculously quick to knit, thanks to the use of extra-large needles. It is an ideal project for a complete beginner, as it uses only one simple stitch and any slight mistakes will be disguised by the textured yarn. Although light in weight, it feels really warm, and is deliciously soft to wear. Make it in any color you like, and experiment with the size–a wider version would make a lovely wrap, for example. In fact, as it's so easy to knit, you could make several to go with different outfits, and it would, of course, make an ideal gift.

gossamer scarf

1 Even if you are an experienced knitter, practice using the large needles until you have got used to their size and weight and have found a comfortable knitting position. The more confident you feel, the more quickly and easily you will be able to knit. Tie the first casting-on stitch loosely so that you will be able to push the large needle through it. Cast on a further 14 stitches, quite loosely, making 15 in total.

2 Knit one row. Knit the second row, knitting in the end of the yarn from your casting on. Continue to knit every row. If you are a beginner, do not worry too much about the guage, as the needles will compensate for any tight or loose stitches, and if there are any gaps the yarn will fill them.

3 Continue to knit every row, either until you have used almost all the yarn, or until the scarf is the right length for you.

4 Bind off, and cut the yarn, leaving about 6in. Thread this onto a sewing needle and stitch in and out of the knitting to secure. If you have joined two balls of yarn, do the same with the loose ends.

BINDING OFF
Make sure you don't knit to the very end of the yarn, as you will need to leave enough yarn to bind off.

leather place mat

YOU WILL NEED

To make a place mat diameter
8in and two coasters
diameter 4¹/₄in

size 0 (size L-11/8mm) crochet hook

22yd leather thong

Talcum powder

Scissors

Modern crochet practitioners experiment with stitches, yarns, and colors to give an innovative twist to a conventional craft form. These place mats and coasters, for example, use leather thong rather than ordinary yarn or thread, and although their pattern is straightforward, they have a desirably contemporary look which would work well in any interior. Their impact comes from a simple shape combined with a neutral color and interesting surface texture.

Brown leather has been used here, but there are many alternative yarns with which you could experiment. For a complete contrast, why not try raffia, which comes in a range of bright and cheerful colors? The result would suit a country kitchen rather than a sophisticated dining table. Or you could use string, twine, or sisal, all of which would have the required toughness for this type of project and would look lovely made up as mats for indoor plant pots.

leather place mat

1 Cast on 5 chains, then slip stitch into the first chain to make a small loop. As you work, pull the leather tight on each stitch so that it does not become slack. It may help to dust a little talcum powder on the hook so that it slips through the leather more easily. It can simply be brushed off afterward.

2 Work 1 chain, then 11 double crochets into the loop. You will find that you have to stop regularly and manipulate the thong in order to fit in all 11 doubles and even the guage. Slip stitch into the chain to join the circle.

3 Work 3 chains, then 2 trebles into the first double crochet space of the previous row, then 1 treble into the next double space. Continue all the way around, alternating 2 trebles then 1 treble into the double spaces. Slip stitch into the third of the 3 chains in order to join the circle.

4 For the next row, work 3 chains, then 1 treble into every treble space. Slip stitch into the third chain to join. Repeat steps 3 and 4 until you have reached the size you require. Finish by working 1 chain, then double crochet into every treble space. Slip stitch into the first chain, then bind off by winding the yarn around the hook and pull through. Cut. To hide the ends of the thong, manipulate them into the crochet with your fingers.

LOOKING AFTER THE LEATHER
You will need to work quite carefully with leather thong as it may crack if it is bent too hard. To keep the finished place mat supple, you could buff it with soft leather polish, either clear or in the same color as your thong.

fragrant door stop

YOU WILL NEED

*To make a door stop measuring
5^1/$_2$ x 5^1/$_2$ x 5^1/$_2$in*

Tracing paper and soft pencil

Paper

Fabric remnants

Tailor's chalk

Scissors

Pins

Seven squares of fabric (heavy calico is
    ideal) measuring 6 x 6in
    to make the outer bag

Sewing machine and thread to
    co-ordinate with your fabric

Embroidery needle and floss in a
    contrasting color to your fabric

Four rectangles of fabric measuring
    6^1/$_4$ x ^{3}/$_4$in to make the
    handle straps

Iron

Button—about 1in diameter

3^1/$_4$in length of narrow ribbon

Seven squares of lining fabric
    measuring 5^7/$_8$ x
    5^7/$_8$in to make the lining bag

21oz sand

21oz lavender shred the flowers off
    the stems and only use those

A handful of batting about 8in
    square, cut into small chunks

Sewing needle and thread

See templates on page 92

With the vintage, retro, embellished look becoming more and more fashionable, this project really is a piece of home-crafted haute couture. While a door stop may seem a rather prosaic item, there's no need for it to be so, and this version would make a pretty addition to any room or hallway, with the added advantage of its subtle lavender scent.

Use a fairly robust fabric for the outside of the door stop. If you wish, the pieces could be complementary in color rather than matching. Then, for your appliqué, choose smaller pieces that work well as a contrast to your main colors. And adapt the design as you wish: it could be made smaller or larger, for example, without lettering or with different lettering, or with appliquéd flowers all over. Don't worry too much about making it really precisely—as long as it's not messy, its charm is in its hand-made, not-quite-perfect character.

fragrant door stop

1 Copy the "stop" and flower templates on page 92 and transfer onto paper. Cut out and lay onto your fabric remnants. For the front panel, use tailor's chalk to draw around the 'stop' letters and cut out. For the back panel, cut out 12 petals and three flower centers. Cut out a rectangle measuring $2^3/_8$ x 1in to be the background for the word "door."

2 To make the front panel, first mark the position of all your lettering with tailor's chalk on one of the outer squares. Pin the "stop" letters in place and zigzag over them (using pale thread) until completely covered.

3 Pin the rectangle in place and zigzag around the edge to sew it in place. By hand, backstitch the words "that" and "door" in a contrasting color.

4 To make the handle straps, take one of the long rectangles and press ¼in on each long edge toward the center, then fold again lengthwise so no frayed edges are visible. Straight stitch together, along the long edge. Repeat for the other three.

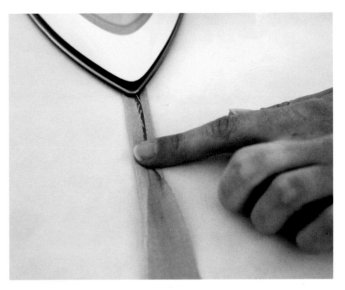

5 Lay the straps onto another outer square (this will be the top) so that they overlap and cross over. Pin and stitch in place.

WHERE TO FIND REMNANTS
As well as leftovers from other sewing projects, you can use remnants of unworn, attractive fabric from clothes, drapes, pillow covers, and so on. Why not hunt around thrift stores and yard sales to pick up pretty pieces that won't cost a fortune.

6 To make the back panel, pin the petals in place on another outer square, with the centers overlapping them slightly. Zigzag around the center then, in a contrast color, the petals.

fragrant door stop

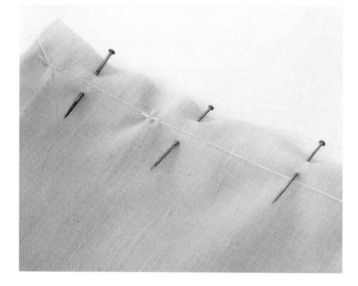

7 To make the outer bag, pin and stitch the front panel to a plain square, right sides together, leaving a 1/2in seam allowance. Pin and stitch a plain square to the other side of the front panel. Then pin and stitch the back panel to either of the plain squares, ensuring that it is the same way up as the front panel, to form a line. Join the line together so that it makes a loop, still with right sides together, and sew the final seam.

8 With right sides together, sew the top to the side pieces, taking care to keep the corners neat, and clipping across them if necessary. Take the two base pieces and fold each of them in half, wrong sides together. With right sides together, pin and stitch onto the sides, ensuring that the two folded edges meet neatly in the center.

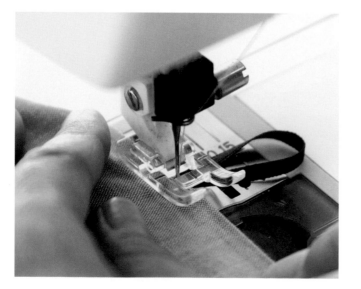

9 Turn out and press. Sew the button to the center of one side of the base. Make a tiny loop using ribbon and sew opposite the button, tucking the ends neatly under the hemmed edge of the base.

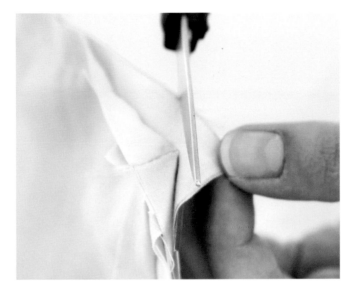

10 To make the lining bag, pin and stitch four squares, right sides together, to form a line. Join together, right sides together, and sew the final seam, leaving a 3¼in gap. Still with the right sides together, stitch the top and bottom pieces onto the side pieces, taking care to keep the corners neat, clipping across them if necessary. Turn out.

11 Fill the lining bag with the mixture of sand, lavender, and batting. Pour the sand in first for weight, then add the lavender, and finally the batting for shape. It might help if you use a container such as a jar or a funnel to pour with.

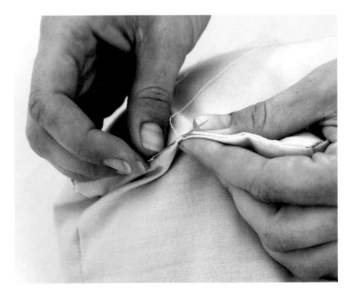

12 When you are happy with the weight and shape of your door stop, hand stitch the gap in the lining bag shut. Put the lining bag inside the outer bag and fasten the button.

rose petal sachet

YOU WILL NEED

*To make a sachet measuring
9¹/₂ x 8in*

72in each of three colors of
ribbon (216in in total)

Scissors

Rectangle of silk measuring 9¹/₄ x 8¹/₄in

Protective mask

Temporary sewing adhesive

Tacking needle and thread

Iron

Pins

Sewing machine

Thread to match your ribbons/silk

1¹/₄oz dried rose petals

For drawers, wardrobes, or storage, a scented sachet is ideal for adding delicate fragrance to your clothes and – depending on the sachet's ingredients–warding off moth. It's a traditional item that has been given an up-to-date twist here by making it from woven ribbons. The result is just as practical, but also really subtle and delicate, with all the prettiness of ever-so-slightly sheer, shiny ribbon.

An ultra-feminine range of pink ribbons has been chosen for this project, combined with a silk backing, but you could create a chic version using, say, taupes or charcoal grays, or a brighter alternative with fashionably clashing oranges and fuchsias, or something sweet and simple in baby-soft pastels. The trick is to choose three different colors that combine really well; after that, the project is very straightforward to carry out, needing little more than an iron, a sewing machine, and a scented filling of your choice.

rose petal sachet

1 Cut the ribbons into 10 lengths of 9¹/₂in and 13 lengths of 8in. Lay the silk, right side down, on a clean, flat surface. Wearing a protective mask, spray the top with temporary adhesive. Lay the shorter lengths of ribbons, parallel with one another, running from left to right across the shorter width of fabric, so that they butt up but do not overlap. Alternate the colors to create an attractive pattern.

2 Lay the longer lengths of ribbons over the first layer, from top to bottom across the longer width of fabric, positioning as before. Baste around one long and one short side to hold them in place. Loosen the ribbons from the adhesive and start to weave them, one at a time, under and over one another. Pull them gently into place so that they are straight and even.

3 Baste the other two sides. Hand wash gently in cold water to remove the adhesive, then press dry.

SCENTS FOR YOUR SACHET
There are a number of lovely scents you could add to the sachet instead of rose petals, including lavender, cinnamon, camomile, mint, and sage.

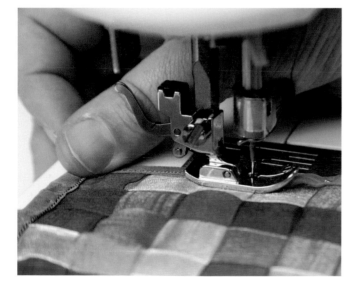

4 Fold over the silk edges of the sachet a tiny amount, press, and pin. Using very small stitches, sew neatly all around, as close to the edges as possible. Remove the basting stitches.

5 Gently ease open the woven ribbons to make a hole and pour the rose petals inside. Pull the weaving closed and straight again. If you wish to hang the sachet, sew a loop of ribbon to one corner.

velvet throw

YOU WILL NEED

White silk velvet, measuring
   $78^3/_4$ x $47^1/_4$in
Scales
Iron
Autofade pen
Needle and basting thread
String (uncolored)
Protective apron, mask, and gloves
Cold-water fabric dye
Large, flat-bottomed bowl
Mixing spoon (cannot be used for
   cooking afterward)
Pins
Polyester satin, measuring
   $78^3/_4$ x $47^1/_4$in
Sewing machine
Thread to match your dye color
See pattern guide on page 94

Shibori is a Japanese word for a technique that involves the shaping of textiles—by braiding, knotting, twisting, or crumpling—and then securing them, by binding, stitching, or knotting, to create a resist before dyeing them. It is a centuries-old technique that creates pretty, softly-edged patterns, which contrast completely with other resist-dyeing techniques involving wax, paste, or stencils, where the aim is to make a sharp, crisp edge.

This shibori project uses a specific technique known as "meander," where you stitch curving lines all over your fabric before gathering them and wrapping with string. It is a very satisfying process, giving a subtle yet rather glamorous effect which is perfectly suited to this slate-gray velvet throw. If you are worried about making something so big on a first attempt, try it out on a smaller piece of velvet and use it as a pillow cover or a scarf—either would be just as attractive and offer an easy introduction to the principles of this appealing craft form.

velvet throw

1 Wash the velvet to remove any finishes, allow it to dry, then weigh, in order to determine how much dye to use. Press on the reverse side. Lay it out flat, right side down, and use the autofade pen to draw curving lines at least 10in apart all over (see the pattern guide on page 94). Hand stitch a running stitch with basting thread along each line, gathering the fabric tight as you go.

2 Bind the gathers by wrapping with string and knotting. Pull the string as tight as you can when you wrap it: if it is loose, dye may bleed underneath and the final effect will be blurred.

USING STRING
Experiment with different thicknesses of string for wrapping your fabric—the thicker the string, the wider the undyed band of fabric. You can also use different thicknesses of thread for the gather-stitching to create a variety of effects.

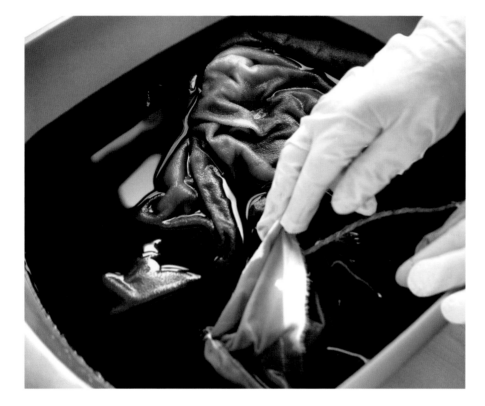

3 Wearing a protective apron, mask, and gloves, mix up the dye in a flat-bottomed bowl according to the manufacturer's instructions. Dampen the velvet, squeeze out the excess water, then immerse it in the dye for at least an hour.

4 Remove the velvet, rinse thoroughly in cold water, and allow to dry. Remove the string and stitches, then press on the reverse side. Pin to the satin backing, with right sides together, and machine stitch along two long sides and one short side. Turn out. Neatly turn in the edges of the remaining side, press, pin them together, and stitch, close to the edge. Press all over.

elegant scarf

YOU WILL NEED

To make a scarf measuring 51¹/₄ x 11in

Hemmed white scarf in very fine
(pongee) silk

Iron

Wooden frame, slightly larger than the
scarf (you can use four battens of
wood nailed together)

About 18 mapping pins (they have a
longer spike than thumbtacks)

About 6 silk pins and elastic bands

Protective apron

Clear gutta – for best results decant into
a small plastic bottle with a nozzle
and screw to a ¹/₃₂in nib

Tissue paper (for practicing)

Water-based silk paints in five colors

Small containers to hold the paints

Size 12 round paintbrush

Dishwashing liquid

See pattern guide on page 94

The technique of silk painting is rapid, versatile and hugely enjoyable–you will get results very quickly and can use any combination of colors to suit your taste. The key to success is confidence, and if you're not used to painting it will really help to practice first, so as to get a good idea of the feel of the gutta nib and the dye brushes in your fingers. Because the gutta outline is slightly raised, it holds the dyes within the lines you have drawn–working on this principle, you can create any patterns you like. You may wish to use the template to start with, and then move onto your own designs once you feel completely familiar with the process.

This delicate scarf is light and feminine, and could be worn as a pretty accessory either during the day or in the evening. If you want to change the size (it would make a sumptuous wrap, for example) simply start off with a larger or smaller hemmed silk rectangle and alter the size of your frame accordingly.

elegant scarf

1 Iron the scarf. Attach it to the frame, using mapping pins on one long and one short side, and the silk pins on the other two sides. The pins should be spaced at regular intervals, and the silk should be stretched taut and even all over.

2 Wearing a protective apron, practice drawing with the gutta on a piece of tissue paper until you feel confident. Don't worry about slight wobbles–they are part of the hand-made effect. The more you practice the easier it will become. When you are ready, draw the outline of the pattern onto the silk using the gutta. Use the pattern guide on page 94 if you wish. Allow to dry.

DRAWING A GUTTA OUTLINE

Draw in continuous, confident lines—a sketchy line will not work. Press the nib firmly onto the surface of the silk to give a good flow of gutta. If you have to stop the line and start again, you will get a small droplet, but this will hardly show on the finished scarf. When using clear gutta, it is hard to see what you are doing, so it helps to place a contrasting color background (a cloth or piece of paper will do) beneath your work.

3 Pour the silk paints into your containers and use them to paint in between the gutta outlines. Work carefully but quickly—don't let the paint dry in patches as this will create watermarks. Make sure that you paint under the pins. Allow to dry.

4 Take the scarf off the frame and iron on both sides to fix the dye. Use the cotton temperature setting and keep the iron moving. Hand wash the scarf, with hand-hot water and a drop of dishwashing liquid, to dissolve the gutta. Squeeze out the excess water and iron dry.

floral place mat

YOU WILL NEED

To make a place mat measuring
  15³/4 x 13in
Paper and pencil
Sheet of acetate
Masking tape
Craft knife
Two rectangles of calico/linen, each
  measuring 13³/4 x 8³/4in
Pins
Sewing machine
Thread to match your fabric
Scissors
Ready mixed, all-purpose craft paints
  suitable for fabric, non-toxic and
  permanent, in two colors
Two small dishes (foil take-out dishes
  are ideal)
Small piece of sponge
Iron
8 sequins
Glue (any strong glue that dries clear)
See template on page 93

Although this printed and stitched place mat appears quite complex, it is actually pretty easy to make. What's clever is the use of different, overlapping fabrics, with a visible raw edge, to create a modern, textural effect, on top of which you print in two colors. There's nothing tricky about this—simply print one color, wait for it to dry, then print the second color through the same stencil. If you wish, you can then move the stencil and repeat the whole process, as shown here.

A neutral base is perfect for the pretty colors used here. Of course, you can vary the colors of both fabric and paint in order to match your dining room or china. The sequin embellishments add a finishing touch, and if you wish you could also add embroidery stitching to the printing to create a truly individual piece of work.

floral place mat

1 Draw your design onto a sheet of paper (or, if you wish, copy the template on page 93). Place a sheet of acetate over the paper and tape it down so it will not move. Using a sharp craft knife, cut out the design to create a stencil.

STENCILLING
When stenciling, make sure the masking tape is stuck down well–it's worth buying a good-quality one. Wait for each color to dry before adding the next.

2 On a clean, flat surface, arrange the fabric rectangles so that one overlaps the other by about 3/4in. Pin, then stitch them together so that the raw edge of the top fabric is visible. If you wish, you can carefully pull some threads out from the edge of the fabric to create an attractive fringed effect.

3 Tape the fabric to a flat surface, right side facing you, making sure that it is taut. Place your acetate stencil on the fabric and secure using masking tape. Pour the first paint color into a dish and sponge through the stencil onto the fabric. Leave to dry and repeat, using a different color and in a different place (if necessary).

4 Iron the fabric, following the paint manufacturer's instructions, to set the paint. Turn over the edges of the mat about 3/8in, pin and hem. Press. If using the template design, finish by gluing sequins to the centers of the flowers.

USING FABRIC PAINT
When stenciling like this, your paint should be a thick consistency so it does not bleed under the fabric. Do not mix it with water.

beaded tie-back

YOU WILL NEED

To make a tie-back measuring 64cm (25in)

Beading needle and thread

1 stopper bead–larger than the others and obviously different in color

Small, sharp embroidery scissors

20g (1oz) size 11 seed beads–this will be the main color "1"

10g (½ oz) size 11 seed beads in a contrasting color "2"

100 teardrop beads

See diagram on page 92

Throughout the centuries, beads have been used for trade, for religious purposes, as symbols of purity, power, friendship or love, and as superstitious objects–to ward off evil or increase fertility, for example. Most of all, however, beads of all shapes and sizes, made from glass, stone, wood, china, or pearls, have been used all over the world for personal and interior adornment, in glorious colors and in a wealth of patterns.

This tie-back (which could equally well be worn as a necklace) has the satisfying quality of looking extraordinarily impressive while actually being really straightforward to make. Though simpler than it looks, it will take a little time, so set aside a few quiet evenings in which to complete it, bearing in mind that you may have to alter its length to suit the thickness of your drapes.

beaded tie-back

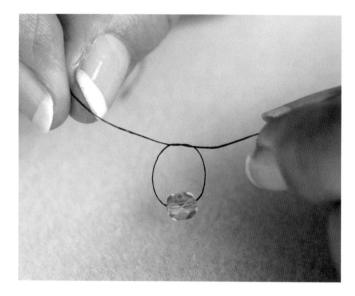

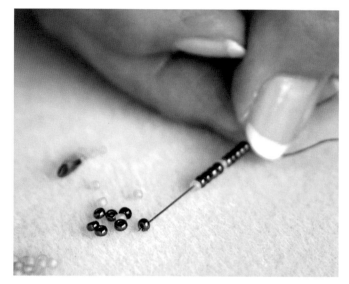

1 Thread the needle with at least 1¹/₂ yards of thread. Start by threading on a "stopper" bead with which to hold the other beads in place, leaving a long tail of thread (you will use this tail in step 6 to make a loop to attach to the wall).

2 Thread on five seed beads in color 1, *one seed bead in color 2, and three seed beads in color 1. Repeat from * three further times. Pick up three more seed beads in color 2, then a teardrop, then two seed beads in color 2.

3 Thread back through bead A (see the diagram on page 92) to start working upward. Thread on three beads in color 1, one in color 2, and three in color 1. Thread through bead B. Thread on three beads in color 1, one in color 2, and three in color 1, then thread through bead C.

JOINING THREAD

To join two lengths of thread, first secure the original thread by running the needle back through your work and knotting it. Run the new thread through the beadwork several times, knot, and continue. Cut the ends neatly.

4 Thread on three beads in color 1, one in color 2, and three in colour 1, then thread through D. You are now working downward again.

5 Continue using this basic pattern until you have used all 100 teardrops or the tieback is the length you want. Ensure that, as you work, you pull the thread firmly but not too tightly—the guage should be the same throughout to make the beads lie evenly.

6 To make the loops to attach to the wall hooks, thread on a row of 60 seed beads in color 1. Turn back, to make a loop, and thread through the 20th bead from the edge of the netting, and then through the rest of this row. Double backward and forward through a few beads to secure the thread, then cut neatly. Repeat for the first end, removing the stopper bead. You will only need to thread on 55 beads this time, as you already have the row of five beads with which you started.

YOU WILL NEED

Three or more large mother-of-pearl
    buttons
Masking tape
Small length of waste wood at least
    3/8in thick
Pencil
Hand drill with 1/16 in/no 53 bit
Three 5/6in jump rings
Flat-nosed pliers
Leather thong

button pendant

It can be quite difficult to make high-quality jewelry
at home, unless you invest in expensive equipment
or enroll on a course to learn complicated
techniques. This project, however, requires simple
do-it-yourself tools that you are likely to have
already, and is particularly easy to carry out,
involving little more than a bit of patience and a
steady hand.

The impact of the pendant comes from the careful
selection of the buttons—if you don't have some
tucked away in a box at home already, you can have
fun hunting them out at thrift stores or yard sales.
Or, of course, you can buy them new. The contrasts
of size and color are especially good here, though
you will probably want to experiment with your own
combinations of shape, size, and number to create a
piece that is both eye-catching and easy to wear, and
totally unique to you.

button pendant

1 Tape your first button to the piece of wood, with the tape partially covering the button. This should hold the button steady and also prevent the drill bit from sliding. With a pencil, mark a hole about 1/8in from the edge of the button.

2 Drill, turning slowly. Do not press too hard or your button may crack. Repeat for the other buttons, bearing in mind that the bottom button needs only one hole but the others will need two, opposite each other.

CUTTING A CENTER HOLE IN A BUTTON

You may wish to cut a large hole in one or more of your buttons, as here. To do this, start by drilling a hole through the center. Take a piercing saw and remove one end of the blade. Insert it through the hole, and re-attach. Carefully saw out a circle, following the center-marking of the button.

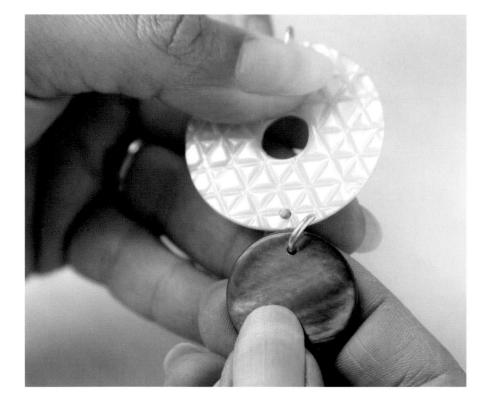

3 Connect the buttons, together with jump rings. To do this, use the flat-nosed pliers to twist the opening of the jump ring sideways, thread through, and close again with the pliers.

4 Add another jump ring at the top of the top button. Cut the leather thong to a length that suits you, and thread it through the jump ring. Tie the ends in a knot.

slate and silver brooch

YOU WILL NEED

Tracing paper and soft pencil
Small piece of thin cardboard
Scissors
Small piece of thin beach-found slate
   (or a piece of tin or silver)
Sharpened masonry nail
Protective apron and goggles
Piercing saw
Jeweler's bench pin (or make your
   own using a slab of medium density
   fiberboard with a notch cut out of
   it. Clamp it firmly to your work table
   with the notch sticking out from the
   edge—to create a space in which
   to saw)
Piece of $^1/_{32}$in thick silver sheet,
   measuring $^3/_4$ x $^3/_4$in
Hammer
Hand drill and $^1/_{16}$in/no 53 drill bit
Needle file
Fine emery paper (or fine wet-and-dry
   sandpaper), wrapped around a
   popsicle stick and secured with an
   elastic band
Flat-nosed pliers
$^5/_{16}$in jump ring
Brooch pin
Two-part epoxy resin
See template on page 93

Much modern jewelry relies for its impact on simplicity of form and subtlety of color, and this project, at once simple and understated, is delightfully appealing. Do not be put off by the sawing and drilling processes—both are safe and easy and, once mastered, will allow you to make and join endless shapes in all sorts of materials.

Here, for example, slate and silver, both tactile materials with beautifully contrasting textures and colors, have been combined. The former, a thin piece of beach-found slate with its surfaces washed smooth by the sea, works wonderfully with the bright, shiny qualities of the sheet silver. If you prefer, however, you could make the entire brooch from silver, with one shape hammered and the other left sleek and smooth. There's also no reason why you shouldn't cut different, graphic shapes or even add an embellishment, such as a glass or pearl bead.

slate and silver brooch

1 Transfer the template on page 93 onto a piece of cardboard and cut out. Lay it onto the slate and scratch around it with a sharpened nail. Wearing a protective apron and goggles, use the piercing saw to cut out the heart shape. Repeat to cut out the star from the sheet of silver. Use the nail and a hammer to mark the position of the drill holes on the silver, and a pencil to mark it on the slate. Drill both, holding in place with a nail and drilling very gently into the slate to avoid cracking.

2 Smooth all the edges, corners and holes, first with the needle file and then the emery board. Using the emery board on the flat sides, too, will create a really polished finish.

3 With the nail and hammer, make the decorative dots on the silver star.

DECORATIVE HAMMERING
Practise making the decorative dots with a hammer and sharpened nail on a piece of scrap silver. Use a firm and even hammer stroke.

4 With flat-nosed pliers, open the jump ring by twisting the opening sideways, and thread it through the drilled holes in the heart and star. Close the jump ring. Glue the brooch pin to the back of the heart, and allow to set.

layered notecard

YOU WILL NEED

Pre-folded card blanks (size A6) or
   make your own
Colored card, wrapping paper or
   paper decorated with ink stamps,
   in a co-ordinating color
Scissors or decorative punch
Hand-made paper in co-ordinating
   colors
Fine paintbrush
Craft glue stick
Board pin or thick darning needle
Cutting board or cork tile
Craft rivet or paper fastener
Double-sided decoupage foam pads
   (or cut up your own stationery fixers)

From corrugated card to tissue, rag-and-fiber paper to crèpe, the range of interesting and unusual papers on the market today is truly impressive, and once you have started to make your own cards you will quickly amass a collection of papers in varying colors, thicknesses, and textures. By layering a number of contrasting papers carefully, so that their inherent qualities really stand out, you can create a card with real "wow" factor.

This design uses a central shape, either cut or punched, to form the top of a "sandwich" of simple squares. To bring out their texture, their edges are torn and not fully glued down, and the card is made slightly three-dimensional by using foam pads to attach the whole motif to the card. This is an attractive, all-purpose card which can be adapted for any occasion.

layered notecard

1 Cut or punch a central motif from the colored card—it needs to have a diameter of about a third of your notecard. Place the motif on a piece of hand-made paper and tear out a square slightly larger than the motif. Tear two more layers from the hand-made papers, each slightly larger than the last, ending with a square that is about two-thirds the width of the card.

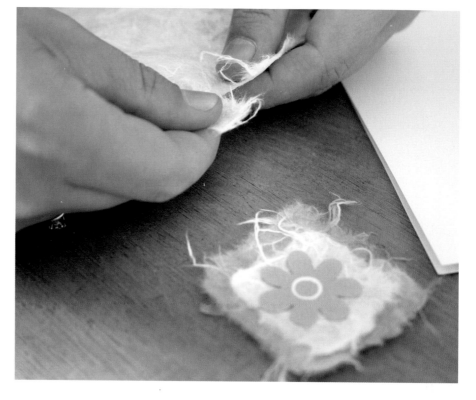

TEARING PAPER
To make it easier to tear the paper, use a fine paintbrush and a little water to paint a line which you can follow when you tear.

2 Glue the layers of paper together, ensuring that the glue doesn't reach quite to the edges so that the layers have texture. Glue the motif to the center of the top layer and allow to dry.

3 Place the cutting board on your work surface. Make a hole through the center of your motif with a board pin or darning needle, and thread the rivet or split pin through. Open out at the back to hold in place. It can be a good idea to slightly open the rivet first to make it easier to open at the back.

4 Turn the design over and attach double-sided foam pads at the corners and middle (covering the rivet), and carefully position over the front of your card. When happy with the position, press down to attach.

wedding stationery

YOU WILL NEED

Selection of hand-made papers in
different weights and textures

Pre-folded card blanks (size A6) or
make your own

Ruler

Craft glue stick

Decorative-edge scissors

Pencil

Small, sharp scissors

Paper or fabric in an accent color

Board pin or darning needle

Cutting board or cork tile

Double-sided decoupage foam pads
(or cut up your own stationery fixers)

See template on page 93

For anyone planning to get married, a beautiful wedding invitation is absolutely essential—and nothing can beat the appeal of a hand-made card, perhaps with co-ordinating orders of service, place cards, and thank-you notes. The obvious motif for such a card is a heart, but this design can easily be adapted to suit your own tastes, while the colors can be altered to co-ordinate with whatever theme you have chosen.

Building on the techniques of the previous two projects, this card has a pretty layering of textures and colors, with a window motif in the center and a delicate tracing of tiny punched holes. While it is not particularly difficult to carry out, it is not a job to be rushed, so if you are planning to make a large number, do set aside plenty of time so that you can achieve a suitably professional result.

Order of Service

Wedding Invitation

Bride

wedding stationery

1 To make an invitation: choose the heaviest paper for the base of your design. Measure the card and tear a square of the paper about two-thirds of this width (see note on page 56 for tearing paper). For the next layer, choose a lighter weight paper and tear a square slightly smaller than the first. Stick the two layers together and set aside to dry.

2 Cut a third square, slightly smaller than the second, using decorative-edge scissors. Fold in half with right sides together, without pressing down on the folded edge (avoid creasing the paper too deeply). Open up and lay flat. On the reverse, use the template on page 93 to draw your heart shape, lining up the center of the heart with the fold. Fold again, and cut out the heart smoothly.

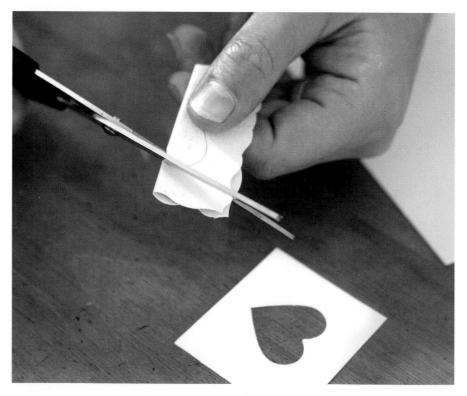

3 Cut a square of accent-color paper or fabric slightly larger than the size of the heart. Apply glue around the outside of the reverse of the heart and stick to the accent paper. Stick this on top of the first two layers and allow to dry. If you wish to use an insert, glue it to the inside of the card at this point.

4 Place the cutting board on your work surface. With the pin or needle, punch holes around the outside of the heart at even spaces. Turn the design over and attach double-sided foam pads at the corners and middle, and carefully position over the front of your card. When happy with the position, press down to attach. If you wish, add a handwritten message on the front. You can make co-ordinating orders of service, place cards, and other stationery using the same technique but different sizes of base card.

memory box

YOU WILL NEED

Acrylic paints in various colors
Container for each colour of paint
Small blank wooden box (not
   varnished)
Paintbrush
Fine sandpaper
Selection of hand-made, natural papers
   in co-ordinating colors (you could
   decorate some yourself – see
   page 65)
Ruler
Scissors
White craft glue and brush
Acrylic varnish
Gold oil pastel
Gilt "treasure" wax
Permanent pen

The craft of collage is as free and inventive as you want it to be. The types of papers you use, their colors and patterns, the sizes and shapes you form with them, the variations in layering–they will all combine to create a unique piece every time. In this project, a blank wooden box has been covered with thinned paint and layered squares of plain and decorated papers. To add to the decorative effect, gold oil pastel delineates the torn edges of the papers and gilt wax enhances the edges of the box. A delightful touch is the repeat of the design on the inside.

Depending on the size of box you choose, you could use it to store photographs, theater programs, vacation mementoes, children's artwork, or any other precious items. The same techniques could also be adapted to cover other containers, such as shoe boxes, box files, or small chests of drawers.

memory box

1 Pour the paints into containers and dilute with water so that they become relatively thin–this will allow the grain of the wood to show through. Paint the box inside and out with your chosen colors. Allow to dry, then gently sandpaper any rough edges.

2 Tear the paper into squares of different colors and decreasing sizes, using a ruler to create straight edges. Cut a simple, graphic shape, too, if you wish (a heart is used here). Arrange in position on top of the box. Tear and/or cut some additional papers to place inside the box.

3 Brush white craft glue all over the reverse of the cut and torn papers. Glue into place. When dry, paint a layer of acrylic varnish all over.

4 Draw around the edges of the papers with a gold oil pastel, then smudge with your finger to soften the line.

5 Apply gilt wax to the inside edges of your box, using your finger.

6 Add handwritten words to the outside of the box using a permanent pen.

PRINTING PAPERS

To make your own decorative hand-made papers (as here), simply use gold acrylic paint and a soft brush to create simple, repetitive patterns such as spirals and dots on hand-made, natural paper.

tea light holder

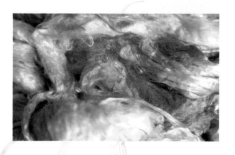

YOU WILL NEED

To make four tea light holders
Mixing bowl
Small pack of cellulose adhesive
3¹/₂oz dyed tussah silk tops
Mold—such as a glass jar, bottle or vase
Plastic wrap
Protective gloves (optional)
Palette knife
Clear wood varnish
Paintbrush

CANDLE SAFETY

These tea light holders are potentially flammable, so only use with tea lights placed within a glass or metal holder, on a stable, non-flammable surface. Keep away from children and pets, and never leave a burning candle unattended.

Working with paper fiber is like a rather more glamorous version of papier mâché—the principle of gluing and layering around a three-dimensional object is pretty much the same, but instead of paper you are using gorgeous silk fibers, which dry to a lusterous sheen and are surprisingly robust. The fibers (called "tops," which simply means a continuous length of combed fiber) are available in a range of appealing colors, though if you wished it would be easy to dye your own.

This technique is not particularly difficult to learn and, while it may take a little practice, the results will be all the more rewarding. The jewel-like shades of the silk looks gorgeous when lit from inside (though bear in mind that you should always be extremely careful with lighted candles), and these pretty accessories are a beautiful means of adding color and interest to a bedroom, hallway, living room, or bathroom.

tea light holder

PREPARATION

Pour a cup of water into a bowl and sprinkle about a teaspoon of cellulose adhesive on top. Do not stir or it will become lumpy. Leave for at least two hours, or preferably overnight, before you start the project. The glue will be clear and turn to a jelly-like consistency.

1 Pull the silk fibers apart by taking hold of the middle of the skein, holding down one end and pulling gently. For one tea light you will need about 24 lengths, which you should lay out separately on your work surface so they are easy to work with. Do not cut with scissors.

2 Completely cover your mold with plastic wrap, and cover this with a generous layer of glue, using your fingers. Wear protective gloves if you have broken or sensitive skin.

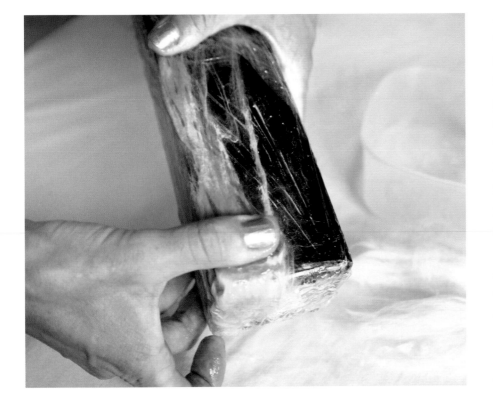

3 Take a length of silk, lay it along your mold and hold the top end with one hand. With the other hand, spread the glue generously along the silk, working up and down with the fibers rather than across them. Use enough glue to penetrate through the fibers, and spread more glue over any areas that have not become translucent. Keep applying the lengths, overlapping very slightly so that the fibers mesh together. Lay two sides over the bottom of the mold to make a base (do not use all four as the base will be too thick).

4 Turn the mold upside down and leave the silk to dry overnight, or use a hairdryer to speed up the drying. It must be completely dry or it will collapse. Use a palette knife to gently loosen underneath the fibers, and prise the tea light holder off carefully. It may be quite difficult to get off at first, but keep going, bit by bit, and it will come eventually. To make the tea light holder more durable, you may wish to cover the outside with a layer of varnish.

pressed-leaf tiles

YOU WILL NEED

About 500g (1lb) self-hardening
  modeling clay—white is best
Newspaper
Two lengths of dowel, two chopsticks
  or two battens of wood that are the
  same thickness
Rolling pin
Skewer
Ruler
Craft knife
A few small leaves (choose hard leaves
  such as ivy or rhododendron)
Medium wide, flat brush and fine,
  pointed brush
Acrylic paints
Palette or white plate
Glaze medium

F or centuries we have been fascinated by our ability to create pottery from the earth. From the elegant urns of Ancient Greece to the great factory-produced wares of the likes of Meissen, Spode, and Limoges, ceramics have played an essential role in our everyday and aesthetic lives. And, despite the potential to dispute whether this is an art or a craft, there is no doubting that making and decorating ceramics is one means of fusing form and function in a satisfying and impressive way.

This project combines the repetitive, geometric arrangement of squares with the organic outline of leaves. The trick is to start by rolling perfectly even slabs of clay, simply by using a guide such as a pair of chopsticks or lengths of doweling. Then you can form impressions using leaves or other textured objects. Either paint over the outlines, as here, or brush the tiles with the same color all over so that the three-dimensional effect is subtle and intriguing.

pressed-leaf tiles

1 Manipulate the clay in your hands to soften it, then work it into a rectangular, flat shape. Lay newspaper on your work surface and position the rolling guides about 7in apart on top. Place the clay between the rolling guides, press flat with your hands, and roll it with the rolling pin. Only roll in one direction as the clay is liable to pucker if you work it backward and forward.

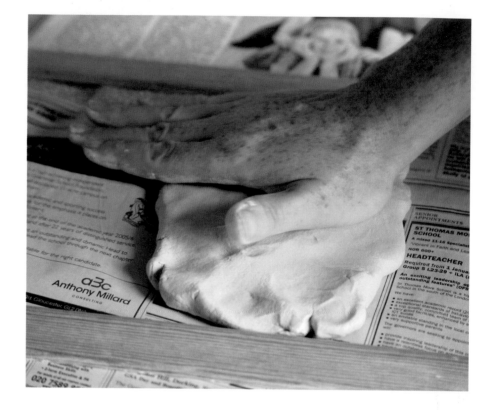

2 Use a skewer (or the point of a pencil) and a ruler to mark out nine 2in squares and cut through the clay with a craft knife. Peel away the excess clay and put in an airtight bag to re-use. Smooth any rough edges of the squares with a little water.

3 Press a leaf onto each tile, pressing quite hard so that it leaves a clear impression of the outline and any veins. Set aside to dry for about 24 hours or speed up the drying process by using a hairdryer on a low-to-medium setting.

4 Cover the tiles with a base coat of white acrylic paint and leave to dry for a few minutes. Paint the impressions of the leaves with a contrasting color. Leave to dry again, then add a coat of glaze medium to give protection and an attractive shine.

DISPLAYING THE TILES
Experiment using different numbers and sizes of tiles, with varying leaf patterns, to create different effects–perhaps a long, thin line, a square, or a random pattern. If you would like them to look more art-like, mount them onto a painted board or in a box frame. On page 71 they are shown mounted onto a textured medium density fiberboard: paint the board with a half-and-half mix of white craft glue and water, lay a piece of cheesecloth on top, smooth and fold over the edges, and paint all over with the glue mix. Leave to dry, trim the edges neatly with a craft knife, then paint.

abstract bowl

YOU WILL NEED

Square, shallow ceramic bowl

Soft pencil or black china marker

Tracing paper (if using the pattern
    guide)

Dust sheet

Protective goggles

Surgical gloves

Overalls, apron, or old shirt

12 x 12in sheets porcelain mosaic
    tesserae 1 x 1in in four colors

12 x 12in sheet glass mosaic tesserae
    ³/₄ x ³/₄in in three colors

Mosaic nippers (spring-action ones
    make cutting less arduous)

Tray with sides

Dustpan and brush

White craft glue

Glue spreader

Tweezers

Rubber gloves

11lb white powder grout

Mixing bowl or bucket

Mixing spoon

Palette knife

Sponge

Soft dry cloth or kitchen towel

See pattern guide on page 94

T he techniques of mosaic have changed little
since uncut pebbles were first laid in simple
patterns to create floors in Ancient Greece. Over the
centuries, it has developed as a craft form that
combines the decorative and the functional in a
powerful way, using cut marble, stone, or glass to
create beautiful images, whether sparse and simple
or complex and dynamic.

To make a start in mosaic you will need to invest in
a small amount of equipment and materials. They
should be relatively inexpensive, however, and it is
almost inevitable that, once you have completed your
first piece, you will want to carry on experimenting
with colors, shapes and patterns. The technique
requires a little practice to perfect, but will yield
good-looking results—such as this impressive
abstract bowl—fairly quickly, and once you have learnt
the basics you will soon be able to adapt them in
order to create your own, original designs.

abstract bowl

1 Either draw a design freehand onto the bowl, using a pencil or black china marker, or copy the template on page 94. Place a dust sheet under your working area then, wearing protective goggles, surgical gloves and overalls or an apron or old shirt, start to cut your tesserae, using a tray to contain the pieces.

STORING MATERIALS

For neatness and efficiency, store loose tesserae in clear containers, and sheets of mosaic in labeled boxes. It is best to keep cements, additives, and adhesives in a cool, dark place until required.

2 Begin by cutting a few of the shapes that you will need to work on the detail of the design, then do more as you need them. Hold the nippers in one hand, toward the bottom of the handle, and a tessera in the other. Place the tessera face up between the cutting edges of the nippers and apply firm pressure. While you are cutting, constantly sweep the tesserae away from you with a dustpan and brush so that you do not cut your hands.

3 Spread the glue to cover small sections at a time and then apply the tesserae, smooth sides up. Work on the small details first, where necessary drawing the shape you need onto the tesserae and snipping along the line. Leave the background until last, filling this in with randomly cut pieces, ensuring that they are evenly spaced. Use tweezers to insert really small pieces. Leave to dry for around 4 hours, or until the tesserae will not move.

4 Working in a well-ventilated room, mix the grout powder with water. Wear rubber gloves if you have sensitive skin. Use the palette knife to spread all over the finished bowl, starting at the center, working between the tesserae. Wipe off any excess with a clean, damp sponge. Clean and polish the mosaic with a soft dry cloth and leave to dry for 24 hours.

leafy mirror

YOU WILL NEED
Craft knife
Self-adhesive plastic measuring at least
    the size of your mirror
Plain mirror to decorate—this mirror
    measured 19 x 12in
Soft cloth, tissue, or kitchen roll
Soft pencil
Tracing paper the size of your mirror
Masking tape
Protective gloves
Glass etching cream
Spatula
Glass cleaner
See pattern guide on page 93

Glass etching techniques can be applied with equal success to a mirror, which is, after all, simply glass that has been backed with metal. Sheet mirror can be bought very cheaply, cut to your exact measurements and used wherever you like, either framed and hung or stuck straight to a wall with extra-strong adhesive.

A quick and easy way to add a beautiful touch of glamour—for a bedroom or bathroom mirror, in particular—is to create an etched pattern using self-adhesive plastic as a resist. Draw on your design, cut away the areas which you wish to etch, apply the paste, wash off, and that's it: a mirror with impact and style. If this project looks daunting, don't worry. You can copy the pattern guide in the back of the book to replicate the pattern exactly, though as you become more confident you may wish to design your own patterns. You could even use the same technique to decorate mirror tiles for a bathroom.

leafy mirror

1 With the craft knife, cut the self-adhesive plastic to the same size as the mirror, and carefully apply it to the front of the mirror, rubbing with a soft cloth as you go to ensure that no air bubbles are trapped. Enlarge the pattern guide on page 93 to the required size. With a soft pencil, draw over the pattern onto tracing paper. Turn the paper over and tape in position over the mirror. Rub over the lines with a pencil, pressing quite hard, so that the design appears on the plastic beneath.

2 Cut the plastic along the pencil line, taking care to cut only the plastic and not scratch the glass. Peel back the plastic to reveal the area to be etched.

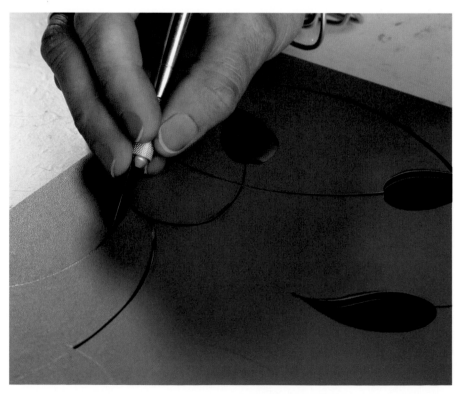

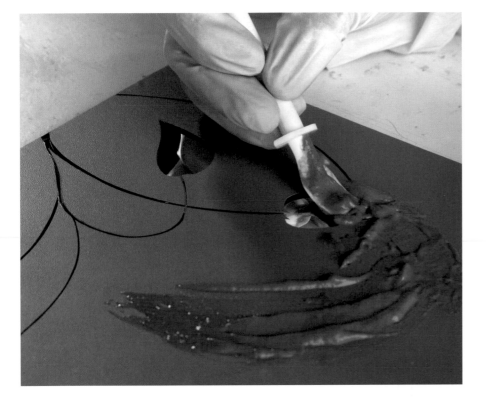

3 Working in a well-ventilated area and wearing protective gloves, spread the etching cream with the spatula thickly over the exposed glass surface. Leave for about 10 minutes.

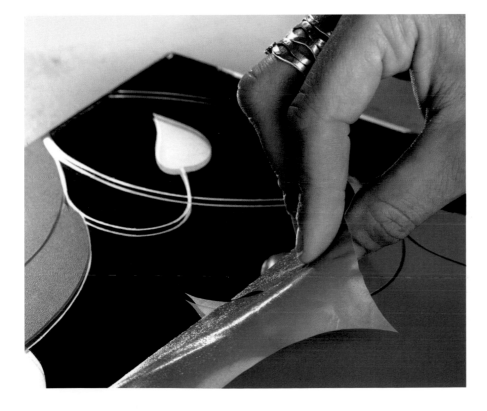

4 Still wearing gloves, scrape the cream back into the pot (to re-use or dispose of safely) and wash off the rest under warm running water. Peel off the rest of the plastic and dry the mirror. Clean the mirror with glass cleaner and a soft cloth.

tips and techniques

knitting–the basics

Holding the needles

There is no right or wrong way to hold a pair of knitting needles–just find the way which feels most comfortable for you. Some people push the ends of the needles into their arm pits while others hold them lower–almost in their laps. It is simply a case of experimenting until you find the way that works best for you.

Getting started

Make a loop with the yarn, then hook another loop through it. Pull gently to tighten and slide the needle through the loop. This is called a slip knot and is your first stitch.

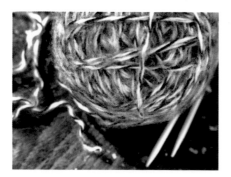

Casting on

Start with the slip knot on the left needle. Push the empty right needle through the loop of the slip knot, from front to back, so that the right needle crosses behind the left needle. Wrap the yarn from the ball around the point of the right needle, from below it to above it. Draw the right needle toward you, holding the yarn on its end, back and out of the slip knot, so that a loop of yarn is pulled through the loop of the slip knot, forming a new stitch.

Note: Please note that these are right-handed instructions. Swap right to left if you are a left-handed knitter.

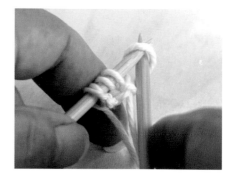

Pass the loop onto the left needle, on top of the previous stitch. Secure the stitch by pulling the yarn, but not too tightly. Repeat, pushing the right needle through the new (top) stitch you have just made.

The knit stitch

Hold the needle with the cast-on stitches in your left hand. Push the empty (right) needle through the

top of the first stitch, from front to back, so that it crosses behind the left needle. Wrap the yarn from the ball around the point of the right needle, from below it to above it. Draw the right needle toward you, holding the yarn on its end, back and out of the cast-on stitch, so that a loop of yarn is pulled through the cast-on stitch, forming a new stitch. Drop the cast-on stitch off the left needle. Repeat until you have reached the

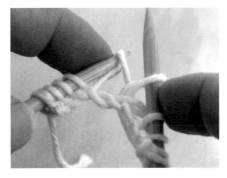

end of the row, then swap your needles into the other hands, so you can start again. Working row after row of knit stitches forms a reversible fabric called garter stitch.

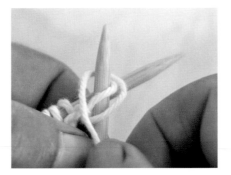

The purl stitch

Hold the needle with the cast-on stitches in your left hand. Make sure that the yarn is at the front of the needle. Push the empty (right) needle through the front of the first stitch, from front to back, so that it crosses in front of the left needle. Wrap the yarn from the ball around the point of the right needle in an counter-clockwise direction, from above to below it, then above again. Draw the right needle toward you, holding the yarn on its end, back and out of the cast-on stitch, so that a loop of yarn is pulled through the cast-on stitch, forming a new stitch. Drop the cast-on stitch off the left needle.

Repeat until you have reached the end of the row, then swap your needles into the other hands, so

you can start again. By alternating rows of knit and purl stitch, you create the most commonly used fabric, called stockinette stitch. The knit rows are considered the right side of the fabric, and the purl rows the wrong side.

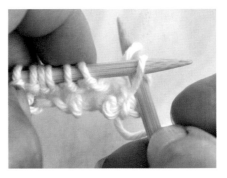

Binding off

Work two stitches, so that you have two stitches on the right needle and the rest of your knitting on the left needle. Push the left needle into the first stitch that you worked on the right needle and lift it over the second stitch and off the needle. Work another stitch, so that you again have two stitches on the right needle, and repeat until you only have one stitch left on the left needle. Pull the yarn through this stitch to secure it.

knitting needle size chart

UK size	US size	Metric
–	Size 19	15mm
–	Size 17	12.75mm
No 000	Size 15	10mm
No 00	Size 13	9mm
No 0	Size 11	8mm
No 1	–	7.5mm
No 2	–	7mm
No 3	Size 10.5	6.5mm
No 4	Size 10	6mm
No 5	Size 9	5.5mm
No 6	Size 8	5mm
No 7	Size 7	4.5mm
No 8	Size 6	4mm
No 9	Size 5	3.75mm
–	Size 4	3.5mm
No 10	Size 3	3.25mm
No 11	–	3mm
No 12	Size 2	2.75mm
No 13	Size 1	2.25mm
No 14	Size 0	2mm
No 15	–	1.75mm

crochet – the basics

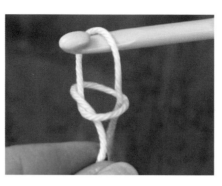

Getting started

Start with the hook in your right hand, holding it as you would a pencil. Use your left hand to control the flow of yarn from the ball. Make a loop with the yarn, then hook another loop through it. Pull gently to tighten and slide the hook through the loop. This is called a slip knot.

Chain stitch

Crochet always starts with a chain stitch, called a "foundation chain." Holding the tail end of the yarn between the thumb and middle finger of your left hand, and with the yarn from the ball held reasonably taut around your left index finger, pass the tip of the crochet hook in front of the yarn, then make a small circular motion with it so that the yarn passes around it. Catch the yarn in the tip of the hook and pull it through the loop of the slip knot that is already on the hook. Pull the yarn gently to tighten. This is the first chain. Repeat, to make as many chains as required.

crochet hook size chart

Please note that hooks sold in the UK and US do not necessarily exactly match the Metric/International Standard Range

UK size	US size	Metric/ISR*
Size 000	N-15	10mm
Size 00	M-13	9mm
Size 0	L-11	8mm
Size 2	–	7mm
Size 3	K-10.5	6.5mm
Size 4	J-10	6mm
Size 5	I-9	5.5mm
Size 6	H-8	5mm
Size 7	7	4.5mm
Size 8	G-6	4mm
Size 9	F-5	3.75mm
Size 9	E-4	3.5mm
Size 10	D-3	3.25mm
Size 11	D-3	3mm
–	C-2	2.75mm
Size 12	C-2	2.5mm
Size 13	B-1	2.25mm
Size 14	B-1	2mm

*International Standard Range

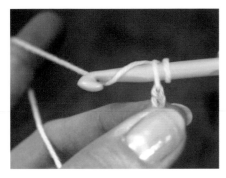

Double crochet

Push the hook through the top of the next stitch. Wrap the yarn around the hook, and pull it through the stitch (but not the loop on the hook). You now have two loops on the hook.

Wrap the yarn around the hook again, and pull it through both loops. NB When making rows of double crochet, you need to work a single chain stitch (called a "turning chain") at the end of each row.

Slip stitch/single crochet

Push the hook through the top of the next stitch (this is usually the second chain from the hook). Wrap the yarn around the hook, as before, and pull it through the stitch and the loop on your hook.

Treble crochet

Wrap the yarn around the hook, and push the hook through the top of the next stitch. Wrap the yarn around the hook, and pull it through the first two loops on the hook. You should now have two loops on the hook. Wrap the yarn around the hook again, and pull it through both remaining loops. When working rows of treble crochet, you will need to make two or three "turning chains" at the end of the each row.

knitting and crochet yarns

Choosing yarn

Yarns can be categorized as either natural or synthetic, with natural yarns made either from animal or vegetable fibers. Animal fibers include wool, mohair, cashmere, alpaca and silk, while vegetable fibers include cotton, linen, and hemp. It is always advisable to buy the yarn specified in the pattern; if you do buy a substitute, try to find one that is the same weight and that has the same guage and fiber content. Check the yardage, as two yarns that weigh the same may have different lengths, so you may have to buy a greater or less amount.

Wool Durable, warm, knits evenly, and neatly.

Mohair Light, delicate, soft, and warm.

Cashmere Soft, luxurious, expensive.

Alpaca Less hairy than mohair; a cheaper alternative to cashmere.

Silk May pill, inelastic, lusterous, and attractive.

Cotton Warm in winter and cool in summer; knits crisply but cheap cottons can droop after washing.

Linen Attractive, knits with a well-defined texture; may be hard to the touch.

Hemp Hard-wearing and highly textural. Too hard for clothing.

Other yarns You can experiment with other yarns for knitting, such as ribbon, leather, metallic yarn, and string.

jewelry-making

A guide to findings

There are, literally, thousands of different types of "findings" (components) with which to complete your jewelry projects, made from solid or plated metal of various types and qualities. Put simply, for necklaces and bracelets (unless large enough to pull over your head or elasticated) you will need an end fastening of some sort, such as a lobster, hook-and-eye, toggle, spring ring, foldover, interlocking, lanyard, magnetic, or screw catch. The style, size, and material will depend on your personal preference and how well it suits the project. When making earrings you will need a pair of hoops, fish hooks, kidney wires, posts, clips, screws, lever-backed rings, or other such base. And for brooches you will need a pin (available in various sizes and styles) and possibly a blank backing. Jump rings are small circles of wire that are used as connectors; split rings are similar but look like tiny key rings, so are more secure but less attractive.

shibori and silk painting

A guide to silks

Silk is a luxurious natural fabric obtained from the silkworm, and is mainly produced in China and Japan. It absorbs dyes easily, producing intense and beautiful colours. There are a range of silks with which it is possible to work.

Charmeuse Matt on one side and lusterous on the other.

Chiffon Shear, extremely light, and has a slight surface texture.

China silk Also known as parachute, pongee or habotai, is the best-known silk and most commonly available. In a plain weave, it is soft, light, smooth, and supple. Inexpensive, versatile, and extremely useful for painting or dyeing projects.

Dupion Quite stiff, with slubbed ribs.

Raw silk Also known as noil silk, is thick, matt, and nubbly.

Satin Heavy, with a very close-weave, and a luxurious finish.

Silk velvet A silk blend with a soft pile on one side.

Twill silk Has a small diagonal rib, making it harder wearing than most silks.

Wild silk Also known as shantung, tussah or honan, it has a pronounced texture and is more irregular than other silks (though all silks have an amount of natural irregularity).

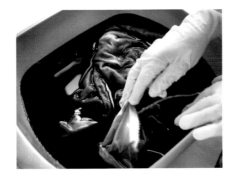

Safe use of dyes, paint and glue etc

Modern craft dyes, glues, and paints are designed to be used by non-professionals at home and are thus generally very safe to work with. However, it is advisable to follow some basic safety rules:

• Keep your working area clean, tidy, and well-ventilated. Do not drink, eat, or smoke whilst using the dyes.

• Protect your work surface.

• Do not use kitchen equipment to mix, prepare, or store dyes, paints or glues, and always store materials and equipment safely. Anything potentially hazardous should be kept in a secure place, out of the reach of children and in clearly marked containers.

• Follow the safety instructions given in the project steps. Wear protective gloves, masks, and clothing as directed, particularly if you have sensitive or broken skin, or suffer from allergic reactions.

• Always read the instructions and the safety information supplied with paints, glues, and dyes, as they may differ from those given in this book. If necessary, consult the manufacturer or supplier for further information.

beading

Types of bead

Beads may be a solid color, transparent, or translucent, gloss, matte or frosted, lustered, rainbow, or metallic. When buying beads it is worth remembering that price usually varies according to quality, and for certain projects it is worth paying more in order to ensure that the beads are regular in size and shape.

Bugle Long, thin cylinders made from glass canes; come in a variety of lengths. Can be straight or twisted.

Cylinder As the name suggests, these are precision-milled cylindrical beads, with a large hole in relation to their size. Also known as Delicas, Antiques, and Magnificas.

Hexagonal Made from six-sided glass cane, these are like a squat bugle bead and appear faceted.

Seed Sometimes called rocailles, these are tiny, round, doughnut-shaped beads, in various sizes, colors, and finishes.

Materials and equipment

Very little equipment is needed to make a start in beadwork, and those that are necessary are inexpensive and easy to obtain.

Magnifying glass Especially useful for threading fine needles and when working with very small beads.

Mat A bead mat has a soft, slightly textured surface to prevent your beads rolling about and make it easier to pick them up with the needle. Make one from felt, velvet, or chamois leather glued to a square of cardboard, and place it inside a tray.

Needles Longer than sewing needles, beading needles have a flat eye to pass through holes in small beads. Size 10 is the largest, and therefore the easiest to thread, but size 13 is smaller, and therefore suited to working with seed beads. They can bend or break quite easily, so it is advisable to buy a number, in both sizes.

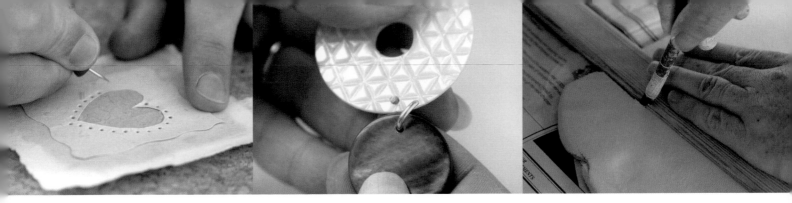

Thread Beading thread is stronger than normal thread, and available in a range of thicknesses and colors. It is a flat thread, and therefore easier to use with a beading needle.

Thread conditioner Will strengthen and protect thread and help avoid knots. Not really necessary for seed beads, but a good idea when working with bugle and cylindrical beads, which can have sharp edges.

Scissors Small, sharp embroidery scissors are ideal.

Thimble Will help protect your fingers when pushing the needle hard through a bead which is already full of thread.

Tweezers Useful for manipulating knots. Fine surgical tweezers are best.

Beginning your beadwork

Before you start, run your fingers along the thread to ease the kinks out of it. You may wish to use a thread conditioner to help avoid tangling. Use as long a piece of thread as is comfortable (about 1-2 yards is best). A "stopper" bead, larger and in a different color to the beads used in the project, can help stabilize your work and prevent the beads slipping off the thread.

Joining threads

From time to time it is necessary to join on a new thread in order to continue working. Leave a tail of at least 6in to make it easier to attach the new thread and weave the end into your work. In dense beadwork, such as brick stitch, weave the new thread in and out off the beadwork several times, finishing by coming out through the same bead as the old thread. Later, weave the old thread back and forward several times and carefully trim off both ends. In more open work, such as netting, tie the two threads together with a reef knot and hide the knot between two beads before tightening it. Weave the ends into your work and cut them off carefully. If necessary, use a small drop of clear nail varnish to make the knot more secure.

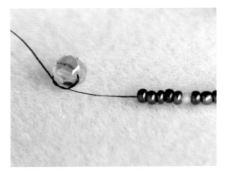

card making and collage

Types of paper
There is an enormous choice of beautiful and unusual papers which you can use for these projects.

Cardboard Available in a range of weights, finishes, and colors. May also be corrugated or textured.

Crepe paper Stretchy paper available in a range of colors.

Embellished paper May be decorated with sequins, beads, stitching, painting, and so on.

Embossed paper Creates an interesting, three-dimensional effect.

Hand-made paper Has a lovely texture and irregularity; may be embedded with leaves, flowers, plant fibers, etc. Many types, including rag-and-fiber, lokta, mulberry, washi, and saa.

Metallic paper Useful for decorative embellishments. Glitter and pearlised papers are also available.

Sandpaper Use for extreme textural definition. Limited colors.

Sugar paper Relatively heavy and rough; good range of colors, economical.

Tissue paper Very light and thin; intense colors.

Velvet paper As the name suggests, the surface of this paper is like soft fabric.

paper fiber

Types of fiber
For our paper fiber project we have specified tussah (wild) silk tops and plant fibers. "Tops" simply means fiber which has been carded, drawn into a continuous length, combed to make the fibers lie parallel and to remove the short fibers, and then wound into a ball. Although it is possible to buy tops in other fibers, using silk gives the desired lustre and translucency for this type of work. The colors are also fabulously vivid–you can buy them ready-dyed, or buy natural fibers and dye them yourself. As for plant fibers, there is a wonderful range to choose from, including bamboo, hemp, flax, linen, jute, and soya bean. Some are thicker and heavier than others, so it is worth experimenting.

mosaic

A guide to tesserae

The pieces used for mosaic can be made from a variety of materials, each with different qualities. They may be supplied in sheet form or loose.

Ceramic Similar to porcelain, except usually comes glazed. It is possible to use household tiles, though do check their durability as they may crack in certain conditions.

Glass and mirror Available from glass and tile suppliers; must be cut very carefully.

Marble Natural colors, polished or unpolished. Need sealing. Marble is cut differently to porcelain, ceramic and vitreous glass tesserae—you must use a hammer and hardie (a small metal block with an anvil-shaped edge) rather than nippers.

Metal leaf Irregular in size and shape, and not durable outside, but excellent for decorative purposes.

Porcelain Usually unglazed, in a wide range of shades. Use indoors and out.

Smalti Hand-cut glass with an irregular surface that reflects light. Heat and frost-proof. Beautiful, but expensive. Use a hammer and hardie to cut.

Vitreous glass Relatively inexpensive; resistant to heat and frost. Available in a range of colors.

Other materials

You may wish to experiment with other materials, such as buttons, coins, shells, beads, semi-precious stones, and found objects such as fragments of china or pebbles.

Cutting tesserae

Wearing safety goggles, cut a few pieces at a time, starting with the colors and shapes that make the detail of the design. To make a circle, cut off the corners of a tile, then "nibble" around the edges in order to produce a smooth, round shape. To make eighths, cut a tile in half, then cut each half in half again. Cut each of these four pieces in half again to make eight small rectangles. Randomly cut pieces should be proportionate in size to the details.

templates and pattern guides

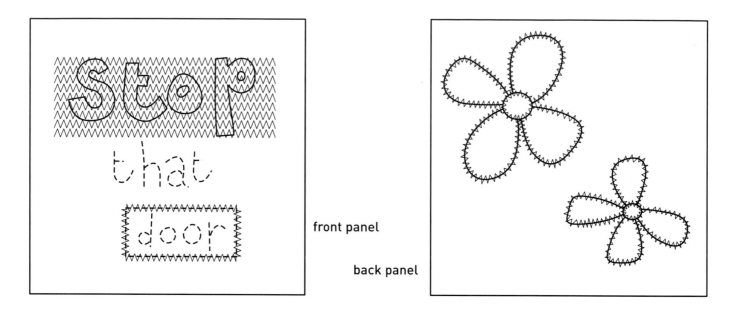

front panel

back panel

page 20 fragrant door stop enlarge to 200%

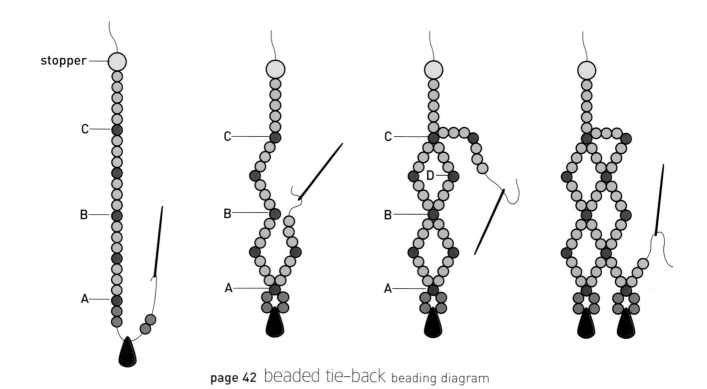

page 42 beaded tie-back beading diagram

page 38
floral place mat
enlarge to 200%

page 58
wedding stationery
trace at this size

page 78
leafy mirror
enlarge to 300%
or use as a guide to suit
the size of your mirror

page 50
slate and silver brooch
trace at this size

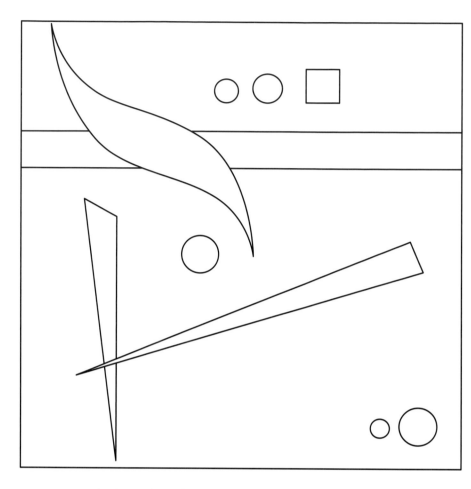

page 74 abstract bowl enlarge pattern to suit the size of your bowl

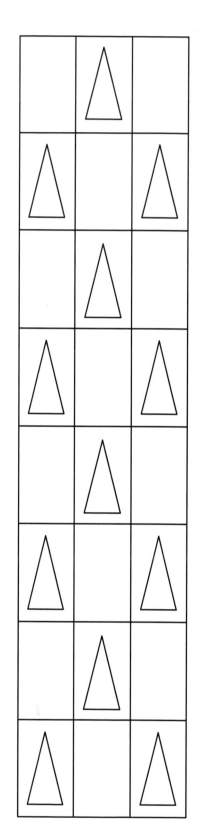

page 30 velvet throw follow this pattern as a guide

page 34 elegant scarf
follow this pattern as a guide

contributors

It may be possible to buy or commission work from the talented craftspeople who devised and created the projects featured in this book. Here are their contact details:

Knitting & Shibori
Jo McIntosh
31 Bedford Road, St Ives
Cornwall TR26 1SP UK
Tel: +44 1736 797122
www.knitweave.co.uk
Email: jo.mcintosh@knitweave.co.uk

Crochet
Jo Stokes
Sparkles,17 Fore Street
St Ives, Cornwall TR26 1AB UK
Tel: +44 1736 795999

Appliqué
Sally Handfield
Up Sticks Boutique
Tel: +44 07866 638600
www.upsticksboutique.co.uk

Quilting & Weaving
Kay Bartlett
Unit 3, Court Arcade
Wharf Road, St Ives
Cornwall TR26 1LG UK
Tel: +44 1736 799424
Email: houseofbartlett@hotmail.com

Silk Painting & Collage
Sally MacCabe
Studio Gallery, 17 The Terrace
St Ives, Cornwall TR26 2BP UK
Tel: +44 1736 799741
Mobile: +44 07885 079902
www.sallymaccabe.co.uk

Printing
Emma Purdie
4 Pounds Park Road
Plymouth, Devon PL3 4QR UK
Tel: +44 01752 706677
Email: emmapurdie@hotmail.com
www.materialgirl.com

Beading
Marion Scapens
Marion's Crafts
26 Richmond Way, Carbis Bay
St Ives, Cornwall TR26 2JY UK
Tel: +44 1736 797623

Card Making
Debbie Whiteman
and Sue Wilkinson
Dandelion Clock Hand Crafted
Cards and Wedding Stationery
20 Penare Road, Penzance
Cornwall TR18 3AJ UK
Tel: +44 1736 366997
Email: dandeclock@aol.com
www.dandelionclock.com

Jewelry
Caroline Kelley-Foreman
Tel: +44 1736 794042

Paper Fiber
Maxine Lunn
Tel: +44 1736 710684
Email: maxisnowi@yahoo.co.uk.

Mosaic
Donna Reeves
Tel: +44 07770 886764

Ceramics
Sarah Sullivan
4 West Street, Penryn
Cornwall TR10 8EW UK
Tel: +44 1326 374682
Email:
ginger@pots.freeserve.co.uk

Glass Etching
Antonia Macgregor
Salt Cellar Glass
Salt Cellar Workshops
Porthleven, Cornwall TR13 9DP UK
Tel: +44 1326 565707
www.antoniamacgregor.co.uk

suppliers

Artbeads.com
Tel: 1-866-715-2323
www.artbeads.com
(Beading and jewelry-making supplies)

Blick Art Materials
Tel: 1-800-723-2787
www.dickblick.com
(Paints, pencils, adhesives, brushes, cutting tools, and other art supplies)

Creative Papers Online
Tel: 1-800-727-3740
www.handmade-paper.us
(Almost 3,000 varieties of hand made and decorative papers)

Dharma Trading Co
Tel:1-800-542-5227
www.dharmatrading.com
(Silks by the yard; also paints, dyes, and other supplies for fabric painting and dyeing)

Factory Direct Craft Supply
Tel: 1-800-252-5223
www.factorydirectcraft.com
(Thousands of discounted craft supplies)

Herrschners
www.herrschners.com
Tel: 1-800-713-1239 for mail order
(Quality supplies for knitting, stitching, papercraft, and others)

Jewelry Supply
Tel: 916-780-9610
www.jewelrysupply.com
(Jewelry and beading materials and tools)

Jo-Ann Stores
Tel: 1-800-525-4951
www.joann.com
(Enormous range of craft supplies)

Josy Rose
Tel: +44 207 537 7755
www.josyrose.com
(Notions for fashion and soft furnishings)

M & J Trimming
Tel: 1-800-9-MJTRIM/212-204-9595
www.mjtrim.com
(Extensive range of beautiful ribbons, buttons, fringing, and other trims)

Michaels
Tel: 1-800-642-4235
www.michaels.com
(One of the US's largest retailers of arts and crafts materials)

Mosaic Supply
Tel: 408-353-8428
www.mosaicsupply.com
(Comprehensive range of tiles, tesserae, and tools for mosaic work)

PRO Chemical & Dye
Tel: 1-800-228-9393
www.prochemical.com
(Dyes, paints, gutta, and other materials for textile design)

Spectrum Glass
Tel: 425-483-6699 for stockists
www.spectrumglass.com
(Manufacturer of specialty sheet glass)

Tinsel Trading Company
Tel: 212-730-1030
www.tinseltrading.com
(Unique vintage and contemporary trims, tassels, sequins, ribbons, buttons, and beads)

Whaleys (Bradford) Ltd
Tel: +44 1274 576718
www.whaleys-bradford.ltd.uk
(Natural fabrics such as silks, cottons, linens, and yarns prepared for dyeing and/or printing)

Wingham Wool Work
Tel: + 44 1226 742926
www.winghamwoolwork.co.uk
(Natural and synthetic fibers)

Yarn Market
Tel: 1-888-996-9276
www.yarnmarket.com
(Wide range of yarns and accessories for knitting, crocheting, and weaving)